EGYPTIAN MYTHOLOGY

MAAT

BY ALLAN MOREY

CONTENT CONSULTANT
KASIA SZPAKOWSKA, PhD
PROFESSOR EMERITUS OF EGYPTOLOGY

Kids Core

An Imprint of Abdo Publishing
abdobooks.com

abdobooks.com

Published by Abdo Publishing, a division of ABDO, PO Box 398166, Minneapolis, Minnesota 55439. Copyright © 2023 by Abdo Consulting Group, Inc. International copyrights reserved in all countries. No part of this book may be reproduced in any form without written permission from the publisher. Kids Core™ is a trademark and logo of Abdo Publishing.

Printed in the United States of America, North Mankato, Minnesota.
052022
092022

THIS BOOK CONTAINS
RECYCLED MATERIALS

Cover Photos: Shutterstock Images, background; Olga Chernyak/Shutterstock Images, Maat
Interior Photos: DEA/S. Vannini/De Agostini/Getty Images, 4–5, 29 (top); CM Dixon/Print Collector/Hulton Archive/Getty Images, 6, 28 (bottom); History and Art Collection/Alamy, 8; Print Collector/Hulton Archive/Getty Images, 9; Shutterstock Images, 10; Mattes René/Hemis/Alamy, 12–13; Arpad Benedek/Alamy, 14; Yulia Ryabokon/Alamy, 15; Chronicle/Alamy, 16, 28 (top); Vladimir Zadvinskii/Shutterstock Images, 17; Sepia Times/Universal Images Group/Getty Images, 18; Ivy Close Images/Alamy, 20–21; Werner Forman/Universal Images Group/Getty Images , 22, 29 (bottom); Zbigniew Guzowski/Shutterstock Images, 25; Smith Collection/Gado Images/Alamy, 26

Editor: Layna Darling
Series Designer: Ryan Gale

Library of Congress Control Number: 2021952340

Publisher's Cataloging-in-Publication Data

Names: Morey, Allan, author.
Title: Maat / by Allan Morey
Description: Minneapolis, Minnesota : Abdo Publishing, 2023 | Series: Egyptian mythology | Includes online resources and index.
Identifiers: ISBN 9781532198694 (lib. bdg.) | ISBN 9781644947777 (pbk.) | ISBN 9781098272340 (ebook)
Subjects: LCSH: Maat (Egyptian deity)--Juvenile literature. | Egypt--Religion--Juvenile literature. | Gods, Egyptian--Juvenile literature. | Mythology, Egyptian--Juvenile literature.
Classification: DDC 932.01--dc23

CONTENTS

Ancient Egyptians wanted to live up to Maat's standards of goodness.

CHAPTER 1

GODDESS OF TRUTH

Maat stood in the Hall of Judgement. She was the Egyptian goddess of harmony and order. She watched as the jackal-headed god Anubis led a dead ancient Egyptian's spirit to her.

The feather of Maat was used in the Weighing of the Heart ceremony.

Maat welcomed the spirit into the Hall of Judgement. It was an important place to her. This was where spirits of the dead were judged.

Inside, other gods waited. They surrounded a large golden scale. Thoth stood to one side, holding a large scroll. He was the scribe of the gods. He wrote down the judgement. Osiris stood to the other side. He was the god of the dead. He judged the spirit.

The person's heart was then placed on one side of the scale. Maat was also the goddess of truth. She held a white feather in her hands. It represented truth and order. She set it on the other side of the scale. If the heart was lighter than the feather, that meant the man had led an honorable life. His spirit would live in paradise forever.

Weighing of the Heart

The ancient Egyptian *Book of the Dead* is a collection of rituals and spells. It told ancient Egyptians what to expect in the afterlife. The ceremonial Weighing of the Heart is one of the many spells in the book. It includes pictures that show each god's role in the ceremony.

The goddess Ammit was also called the Eater of Hearts.

That was the case for this lucky spirit. The side of the scale with his heart rose up. His heart weighed less than the feather. It meant the man had lived up to Maat's standards.

If he had not lived up to Maat's standards, the goddess Ammit would have eaten him. She was known as the devourer of the dead. She had the head of a crocodile, front legs of a leopard, and rear legs of a hippo. Once she ate the souls' hearts, their spirits disappeared forever.

Weighing of the Heart Ceremony

Maat
the goddess of truth

Anubis
the guide of dead spirits

feather of Maat

Osiris
the judge of the dead

Thoth
the scribe of the gods

Egyptian gods and goddesses had different roles in the Weighing of the Heart ceremony. Anubis guided the spirit to the ceremony. The spirit's heart was weighed against the feather of Maat. Thoth would record the judgement. Then, if the spirit's heart was lighter than the feather, the spirit would join Osiris in the afterlife.

Myths played an important role in the ancient Egyptian civilization.

Egyptian Mythology

The ancient Egyptian **civilization** began about

5,000 years ago. Myths played an important

role in ancient Egyptians' lives. These stories helped them understand the world around them. Myths told how the world came to be.

Ancient Egyptians believed that Maat was partly responsible for natural events. She played a role in the sunrise and weather. Myths about Maat helped ancient Egyptians lead good lives.

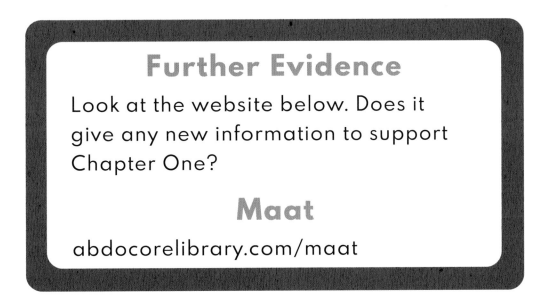

Further Evidence

Look at the website below. Does it give any new information to support Chapter One?

Maat

abdocorelibrary.com/maat

In some myths, the god Ra, *left*, brought Maat, *right*, with him as he created the world.

CHAPTER 2

MYTHS OF MAAT

Maat was the daughter of Ra, the sun god. He ruled over the world and all the other gods. Ancient Egyptians believed Maat played an important role in the creation of the world. According to some myths, she was present when Ra made the universe.

Ra, often shown as a falcon, created the world to have harmony.

Creation Myth

In the beginning, there was nothing but dark, swirling waters of **chaos**. From these waters came Ra. In some myths, Ra created himself. He rose from Earth on his sun boat. This boat, also called a bark, could sail through the sky.

Maat provided order to Ra's creation.

Ra brought Maat with him. He and Maat are among the oldest gods in Egyptian mythology. Ra made the world to live up to Maat's standards. Maat represented everything right with the world. She also represented harmony.

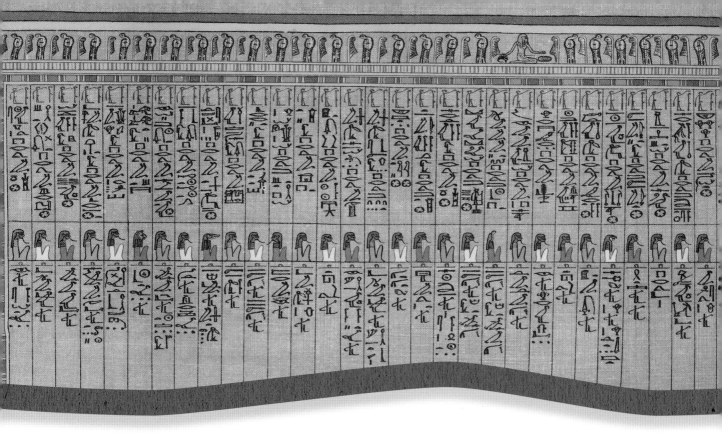

Forty-two gods helped judge the spirit during the Weighing of the Heart ceremony. Many of them are shown here.

If the sun rose and set, there was harmony. The order Maat provided kept everything from falling back into the chaotic waters.

The 42 Judges

Forty-two gods watched Anubis lead spirits into the Hall of Judgement. These gods were

In some myths, the god Thoth was *Maat's husband.*

not as well-known as Maat. But they played

an important role in the Weighing of the Heart.

They sat in the Hall to help judge the spirits.

Thoth

Some myths say that Maat was married to Thoth. Thoth was the god of writing and the moon. He was a master of knowledge and created the calendar. Thoth was also the scribe of the gods. He recorded the results at the Weighing of the Heart ceremony.

The feather of Maat is shown here with the god Thoth.

Each spirit spoke to these gods as their heart was being weighed. The spirit would make **statements**. The spirit told one god they had not stolen. They told the next god they had not lied. Maat's feather helped judge the truth of these statements. When the spirit spoke the truth, their heart would be lighter than the feather. But if the spirit lied, the heart would be heavier.

The *Book of the Dead* describes the Weighing of the Heart ceremony. In it, the spirit being judged says:

> I have not caused pain.
>
> I have not caused weeping.
>
> I have not killed.

Source: W. K. Simpson. *The Literature of Ancient Egypt: An Anthology of Stories, Instructions, Stelae, Autobiographies, and Poetry.* Yale University, 2003. 269.

What's the Big Idea?

Read this quote carefully. Does it support the information in this chapter or give a different perspective? Explain how in a few sentences.

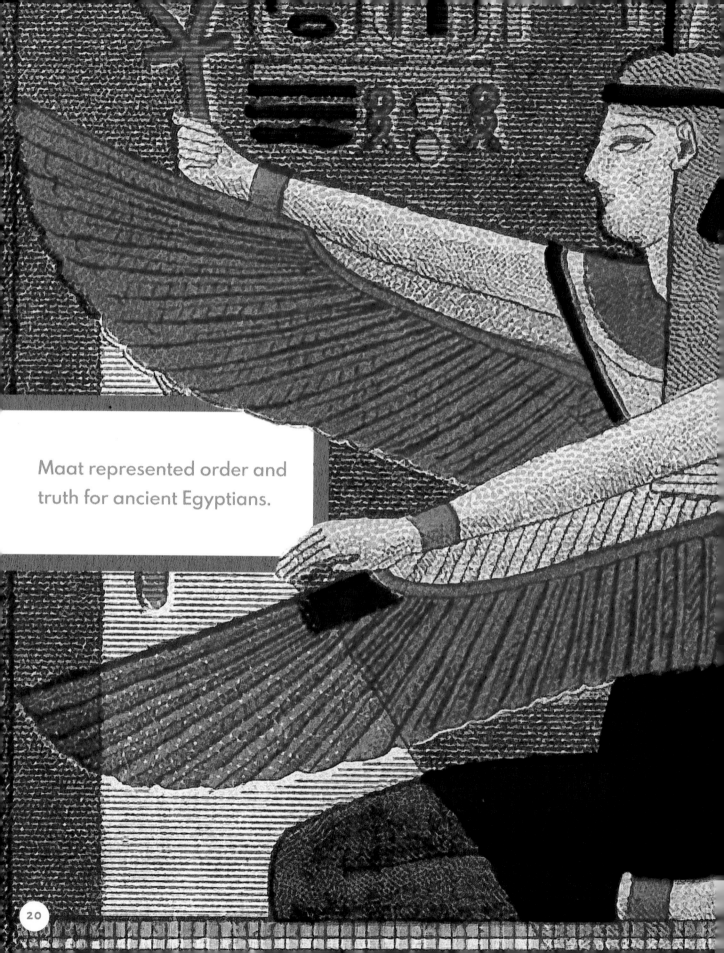

Maat represented order and truth for ancient Egyptians.

CHAPTER 3

MAAT IN ANCIENT EGYPT

To ancient Egyptians, Maat was more than a goddess. She represented a way of life. Egyptians wanted to live in ways that would please Maat. She was a symbol of truth and order. They wanted their society to be as good and just as her.

In art, Maat often wears a white feather on top of her head.

They believed it helped them reach the paradise of the afterlife.

Maat in Art

Unlike many ancient Egyptian gods, Maat is shown with a human head. Sometimes she has wings under her arms. Most often she is shown wearing a headdress with a single white ostrich feather. This feather is used in the Weighing of the Heart ceremony. It also represents her name. Egyptians wrote with images that represented words or sounds. A feather is the symbol of Maat.

Ancient Egyptian **tombs** included images of Maat because of her role in the journey to the afterlife. She is often carved into coffins.

Plinth

A plinth is a symbol of Maat. A plinth is the foundation, or base, of a throne. Like a plinth supports and holds up a throne, Maat was the foundation of Egyptian society.

Paintings and carvings of her are seen on tomb walls and doorways. In art, she is shown performing scenes from the *Book of the Dead.*

New Kings

Maat played a role in new rulers coming to power. Ancient Egyptians thought a king's most important task was to keep the order created by Maat. They believed their rulers needed to support truth and justice. Otherwise the world would fall back into chaos.

Egyptian kings from the New Kingdom period (1500s–1000s BCE) honored Maat through **monuments** and temples. During this period, the kings focused on building temples with balance and **symmetry**. These

The Karnak Temple is an example of the balance and symmetry common to New Kingdom temples.

were places for Egyptian kings to give and receive offerings. This helped to keep order in the afterlife.

Ancient Egyptians honored Maat by living their lives up to her standards.

Worship of Maat

Ancient Egyptians did not worship Maat as they did other gods. They did not build large temples dedicated to her. Instead, they built shrines honoring her in the temples of other gods. Most of all, they honored her by living by the ideas of truth and justice that she represented.

Ancient Egyptians saw Maat as a part of everything. She kept the world in harmony and order. They believed that by following her guidance, balance would be maintained throughout the world.

Explore Online

Visit the website below. Does it give any new information that wasn't in Chapter Three?

Deities in Ancient Egypt—Ma'at

abdocorelibrary.com/maat

LEGENDARY FACTS

The *Book of the Dead* is a collection of spells and rituals. It told ancient Egyptians what to expect in the afterlife.

Maat welcomed spirits into the Hall of Judgement for the Weighing of the Heart ceremony.

Maat was a part of everyday life for ancient Egyptians. They honored her by living truthful lives.

Ancient Egyptians thought a king's most important task was to keep the order created by Maat.

Glossary

afterlife
in ancient Egypt, a place where a person's spirit goes after death

chaos
disorder and confusion

civilization
a complex, organized society

monuments
buildings, stones, or statues that honor people or events

statements
sentences stated in words that are not questions

symmetry
balanced proportions

tombs
burial chambers for people who have died

Online Resources

To learn more about Maat, visit our free resource websites below.

Visit **abdocorelibrary.com** or scan this QR code for free Common Core resources for teachers and students, including vetted activities, multimedia, and booklinks, for deeper subject comprehension.

Visit **abdobooklinks.com** or scan this QR code for free additional online weblinks for further learning. These links are routinely monitored and updated to provide the most current information available.

Learn More

Bell, Samantha S. *Ra*. Abdo, 2023.

Honovich, Nancy. *1,000 Facts about Ancient Egypt.* National Geographic, 2019.

Index

About the Author

Allan Morey grew up on a farm in central Wisconsin. That is where he developed his love for animals and the outdoors. Morey received a Master of Fine Arts degree from Minnesota State University, Mankato, and he has written dozens of books for children. He now lives in Saint Paul, Minnesota, with his wife and their many furry family members.